LEARN RUBY IN 7 DAYS

Nitin Kore

Pune, India

Copyright and license

Learn Ruby in 7 Days: Copyright © 2017 by Nitin Kore.
Last updated 2017/10/08 05:30:00 IST.
All source code in this book is available under the MIT License.

The MIT License

Permission is hereby granted, free of charge, to any person obtaining a copy of this software and associated documentation files (the "Software"), to deal in the Software without restriction, including without limitation the rights to use, copy, modify, merge, publish, distribute, sublicense, and/or sell copies of the Software, and to permit persons to whom the Software is furnished to do so, subject to the following conditions:

The above copyright notice and this permission notice shall be included in all copies or substantial portions of the Software.

THE SOFTWARE IS PROVIDED "AS IS", WITHOUT WARRANTY OF ANY KIND, EXPRESS OR IMPLIED, INCLUDING BUT NOT LIMITED TO THE WARRANTIES OF MERCHANTABILITY, FITNESS FOR A PARTICULAR PURPOSE AND NONINFRINGEMENT. IN NO EVENT SHALL THE AUTHORS OR COPYRIGHT HOLDERS BE LIABLE FOR ANY CLAIM, DAMAGES OR OTHER LIABILITY, WHETHER IN AN ACTION OF CONTRACT, TORT OR OTHERWISE, ARISING FROM, OUT OF OR IN CONNECTION WITH THE SOFTWARE OR THE USE OR OTHER DEALINGS IN THE SOFTWARE

Dedicated to

My Parents
I'm proud to dedicate this book to my parents, who taught me the importance of sharing and the happiness associated with it. With this book, I am sharing my vast knowledge and experience (acquired over 18 years) in Ruby to people who are interested in learning the language.

***"Knowledge is not power, the Sharing of knowledge is power"** –*
Douglas Merrill

Acknowledgments

I would like to express my sincere gratitude to each and every one who helped me write this book, especially my lovely sisters who were the real inspiration behind coming up with the idea of writing it. I would also like to convey my special thanks to all the staff members (especially Pramod and Sanyogita) in KORESOL SOFTWARE LLP. It was them who worked hard in providing real-life practical examples for this book.

Many thanks to Mr. Suzuki Masahiro – san for being my mentor for decades, and guiding me at every professional step, including writing this book.

"LEARN RUBY IN 7 DAYS" owes to Mr. Nitin Soni, who guided and supported me to provide better shape to it. Without his guidance, my journey of writing this book would have been extremely difficult.

I would like to acknowledge long list of my mentors, seniors and friends (who directly or indirectly contributed) from various places I stayed, studied, worked or associated with. Just to name a few – Infosys, Cognizant, TCS, CMC, Polaris, COEP, SEED Infotech Pune, LTRV School, BNI Champs Pune, J4E Entrepreneurs group, deAsara, S&P, Citibank, Barclays, BNY, Fidelity, Amex and ABN Amro. I gratefully acknowledge their help, support, and love.

Last but not the least – all the reviewers and editors of this book (especially Rahul Khandelwal, Sarvesh Joshi, Pritesh Joshi), who helped me to make this book more concise, practical and useful.

About the Author

Nitin Kore is the Founder and CEO of KORESOL SOFTWARE LLP and has formerly worked with many MNC's like Infosys, TCS, Cognizant, Polaris, and CMC before starting his own company KORESOL. He has completed his Bachelor of Engineering (B.E.) from COEP – Pune University. He has about two decades of experience in the field of Information Technology. He also has a vast experience in serving many Fortune 500 clients like Citibank, Fidelity, S&P, BNY to name a few. Nitin always had a vivid passion to give back to the society, and this passion led him to come up with this quick guide for Ruby programmers that would help them understand the widely used concepts in Ruby. These concepts are also important for anyone who wants to learn Ruby on Rails framework.

Preface

The basic idea behind writing this book is to provide a simple to understand guide to people who are willing to learn this beautiful language Ruby easily and quickly. The book is written to explain each and every concept in an easy and lucid language along with examples clearly stated.

Table of Contents

DAY 1	1
DAY 2	9
DAY 3	23
DAY 4	35
DAY 5	45
DAY 6	55
DAY 7	73
UPCOMING RAILS TUTORIAL	81

DAY 1

Ruby Introduction

Ruby Installation

First Ruby Program

DAY 1

Ruby Introduction

Ruby was launched in 1990 by Yukihiro Martz Matsumoto. It is flexible and easy to learn programming language. It is also a dynamic, completely object-oriented and open source programming language that supports all kind of platforms including Windows, Mac OS and all versions of UNIX. Ruby considers everything as an object. We will learn more about classes and objects in later sections.

Programmers willing to learn Ruby on Rails framework should first learn Ruby. They could treat this book as a guide and prerequisite before start learning Ruby on Rails framework. Many popular websites like Twitter, Shopify, Airbnb, Hulu, Basecamp, Disney, and GitHub have been developed using this framework. There is a lot of demand for people experienced in Ruby on Rails framework.

Who is the target audience?
- Anyone who wants to learn coding quickly - Ruby is built with programmer's happiness in mind
- Anyone who wants to start their career as a software programmer
- Anyone who wants to develop web applications using Ruby on Rails framework must first learn Ruby
- Anyone who wants to start their startup in software space

What will you learn?
- Building Ruby based software programs
- Ruby language syntax
- Handling conditional statements, loops, iterators, math functions, strings
- Handling exceptions, arithmetic operators, yield, blocks
- Handling arrays, hashes, variables, and scopes
- Writing object-oriented concept based programming
- Start building real-life programs in Ruby

Features of Ruby

Object oriented
    Ruby is a complete object oriented programming language.
Flexibility
    Ruby is a flexible language as you can easily add, remove, or redefine the existing parts of this language.
Case sensitive
    Ruby is a case-sensitive language as lowercase letters, and uppercase letters are completely different.

Statement delimiters
    Multiple statements on one line must be separated by semicolons (;), but they are not required at the end of a line; a linefeed is treated like a semicolon. If a line ends with a backslash (\), the linefeed

following it is ignored; this allows you to have a single logical line that spans several lines.

Ruby Installation

There are various ways to install Ruby or use Ruby over the cloud. Below mentioned are four different methods to make Ruby available for your practice. However, you can explore other suitable methods available on the Internet.

Method1 - On book's website console
We created complementary website console for your Ruby practice. This webpage is available at URL below:
https://books.koresol.com/rubyconsole
Once you open the above page, just start practicing Ruby in the provided web console.

Book codebase
All code snippets mentioned in this book are available at *github* URL below:
https://github.com/koresol/learn-ruby-in-7-days

Method2 - Rails Installer
Visit Rails Installer downloads web page available at URL - http://railsinstaller.org/en. The latest installers are available at the bottom of the page; please install required version. The code snippets explained within this guide have been tested on Ruby version 2.3.3

Method3 - Ruby Installer
Visit Ruby Installer downloads web page available at URL - http://rubyinstaller.org/downloads. The latest installers are listed on

the top left column of the page for each major version of Ruby. Below web pages will also be helpful while installing Ruby from Ruby Installer website:

https://github.com/oneclick/rubyinstaller/wiki/Development-Kit
https://rubyinstaller.org/2017/05/25/rubyinstaller-2.4.1-1-released.html

Method4 - C9 Cloud

There are many *cloud based ready Ruby on Rails environments* available. *http://c9.io* is one of them. To use this cloud - Sign up for a Cloud9 account at *http://c9.io*. Once you sign in, you'll be prompted to create a new workspace. A workspace is basically a coding environment. Select Ruby on Rails workspace, set a project name and create the workspace. Once your Rails workspace is created, you will be provided with Terminal (similar to Terminal in Linux) at the bottom of the screen, after you open the workspace. You can practice your Ruby program within this terminal window.

First Ruby Program

Let us create a small welcome program using Ruby. By convention, Ruby source files have the *.rb* file extension.
1. Use any text editor (e.g. Sublime, Textpad, Vim, Notepad++ etc.) and create a *koresol.com-first_ruby_program.rb* file and write the following code in that:

```
puts  "Welcome To Koresol's Ruby Tutorial."
```

2. Make sure to note the *file and folder path* where you save this file. E.g., above written program is a ruby file - **koresol.com-first_ruby_program.rb** saved in a *koresol folder* in *D:\drive*. Throughout this tutorial, we'll be saving all files in this folder only. In later code samples, we will use $ sign to represent folder path *D:\koresol*. Irrespective of the platform (Linux, MAC or Windows) you use, these instructions will work seamlessly.

Now, let's open the command prompt (or terminal in Linux or MAC OS) and change directory to the path where you saved your ruby file, as shown below:

```
C:\Program Files\PowerCmd>d:
D:\>cd koresol
D:\koresol>
```

3. Now execute the ruby file with the command *ruby filename* and you would see the output as:

```
D:\koresol> ruby koresol.com-first_ruby_program.rb
Welcome To Koresol's Ruby Tutorial
```

Note: Ruby is a scripting language. There is no special main method in Ruby from where execution begins. The Ruby interpreter is given a script of statements to execute, and it begins executing at the first line and continues to the last line.

DAY 2

puts And gets

Variables And Assignment

Conditional Statements

DAY 2

puts And gets

P*uts (s* in puts stands for the string; puts really means *put string)* simply writes onto the screen whatever comes after it, but then it also automatically goes to the next line. We've already studied about using the "put" string to display some data, and the next step is to study the use of "get" string. Similarly to "puts" the ruby method for getting input is "gets." In this sample *koresol.com-gets_puts.rb* we ask the user to enter their company name. It is pretty simple to remember *puts* and *gets* where puts provide information to the user and gets is to collect some information.

Example:

```
Path => /koresol.com-gets_puts.rb
print ( 'Enter your company name: ' )
name = gets()
puts ( "Welcome To #{name}" )
```

Output: Now execute the above ruby file and you would see the output as:

```
$ ruby koresol.com-gets_puts.rb
Enter your company name: Koresol Software LLP
Welcome To Koresol Software LLP
```

Seems simple right, but there are still a few details that you need to understand clearly here. When you look at the program carefully, you can see instead of puts; I've used print. This is because I need the cursor to remain on the same line, as puts add a linefeed at the end whereas print does not. In the next line, I've used gets () to get some information from the user, and that information collected from the user is assigned to a variable. You don't need to initialize a variable in ruby nor do you need to specify its type in Ruby as you can create variables whenever needed and Ruby identifies its type based on how it is associated. In this case, the variable is assigned to a string, and hence Ruby understand that the name variable must be a string.

Variables And Assignment

To store a number or a string in your computer's memory for use later in your program, you need to give the number or string a name. Programmers often refer to this process as an assignment, and they call the names variables. A variable springs into existence as soon as the interpreter sees an assignment to that variable.

Example:

```
Path => /koresol.com-variables_assignment.rb
company = "Koresol Software LLP"
quantity  =   4
# Defining a constant  PI
PI = 3.1416
puts PI
name = "My company web url is www.koresol.com"
product  =  " Develop Eccomerce Webisite"
 puts product
price = 5
cost   =   '2'
puts price + cost.to_i
```

Output: Now execute the above ruby file, and you would see the output as:

```
$ ruby koresol.com_variables_assignment.rb
3.1416
Develop
Eccomerce Website
7
```

Types of variables
There are four types of variables in Ruby:
Local variables
Class variables
Instance variables
Global variables

Local variables
The name of the local variable either starts with a lowercase letter or an underscore (_). It has only a limited scope and can be accessed only inside the block it has been initialized. It has no scope out of the block or function. When you reference or call an uninitialized variable, it could be interpreted as a call to a method without any arguments.
Example:
localvariable1 = 50
_Localvariable2 = 100

Class variables
A class variable is a variable that belongs to the whole class and can be accessed from anywhere within the class. Any changes made to the value of the class variable will affect every instances where it has been referenced. These variable names start with **@@** sign and need to be initialized before it is used or will result in an error. The class variables are common to the class and shared by all instances.

Example:

```ruby
Path => /koresol.com-class_variable.rb
class  Company
   @@no_services=0
      def  initialize(service_name)
         @service_name= service_name
         @@no_services += 1
      end
      def  total_no_of_services()
         puts "Total services: #@@no_services."
      end
end
# Create Objects
service_first = Company.new("Eccomerce Website ")
service_second = Company.new("Android Application ")
service_third = Company.new("iOS Application ")
service_fourth = Company.new("iPhone Application ")
# Call Methods
service_first.total_no_of_services()
service_second.total_no_of_services()
service_third.total_no_of_services()
service_fourth.total_no_of_services()
```

Output: Now execute the above ruby file, and you would see the output as:

```
$ ruby koresol.com-class_variable.rb
Total services: 4
Total services: 4
Total services: 4
Total services: 4
```

Instance variables

An *instance* variable is a variable that has limited access to a particular instance of a class. It is similar to a class variable, but the only difference is that an instance variable has a separate copy for each instantiated object of the class. You don't need to initialize an instance variable and will have a nil value if not initialized. An *instance* variable name starts with @ sign.

Example:

```
Path => /koresol.com-instance_variable.rb
class Company
   def initialize(service_name)
      @service_name = service_name
   end
   def display()
      puts "Service name #@service_name"
   end
end
# Create Objects
service_first = Company.new("Eccomerce Website")
service_second = Company.new("Android Application")
# Call Methods
service_first.display()   service_second.display()
```

Output: Now execute the above ruby file, and you would see the output as:

```
$ ruby koresol.com-instance_variable.rb
Service name Eccomerce Website
Service name Android Application
```

Global variables

A global variable is a variable that has a global scope, means it can be accessed from anywhere within the program. When uninitialized, these global variables have a nil value, and it is generally not recommended to use these global variables as they make it pose a security threat as global data can be accessed from anywhere in the program. Ruby comes with a lot of predefined global variables.

Example:

```
Path => /koresol.com-global_variable.rb
$eccomerce = "Koresol"
class   Product
  def display
      puts "Product's variable is #$eccomerce"
  end
end
class Order
  def display
      puts "Order's variable is #$eccomerce"
  end
end
product = Product.new
product.display
order = Order.new
order.display
```

Output: Now execute the above ruby file, and you would see the output as:

```
$ ruby koresol.com-global_variable.rb
Product's variable is Koresol
Order's variable is Koresol
```

Conditional Statements

Ruby if-else statement

Similar to *if-else* conditions used everywhere, the Ruby *if-else* statements are also used to test a particular condition. There are various types of *if* statements in Ruby:

- if statement
- if-else statement
- if-else-if (elsif) statement
- ternary (shortened if statement) statement

Ruby if statement

The basic *if* statement where the code inside the *if* block executes if the condition is true

Syntax:
    if (condition)
       //code to be executed
    end

Example:
```
Path => /koresol.com-if_loop.rb
puts "Enter price"
price = gets.chomp.to_i
if price >= 100
    puts "You will get product."
end
```
Output: Now execute the above ruby file, and you would see the output as:

```
$ ruby koresol.com-if_loop.rb
Enter price
200
You will get product.
```

Ruby if else

Similar to the *if* statement where a condition is tested. But the only difference here is that the *if* block executes if the condition is true or the *else* block statement is executd.

Syntax:
    if(condition)
      //code if condition is true
    else
      //code if condition is false
    end

Example:

```
Path => /koresol.com-if_else.rb
puts "Enter price"
price = gets.chomp.to_i
if price >= 100
    puts "You will get product."
else
    puts "You will not get product."
end
```

Output: Now execute the above ruby file, and you would see the output as:

```
$ ruby koresol.com-if-else.rb
Enter price
50
You will not get product.
```

Ruby if else if (elsif) statement

The Ruby *if else if* statement is another type of Ruby *if-else* statement, where you may be in need of certain cases that you need to execute certain block of statements based on multiple conditions. This is where the Ruby *if else if* statement comes handy.

If the condition in the *if* block statement is true then code in that block gets executed, or it moves to the *elsif* block and sees if the condition is true there and executes the code there or it moves over the *else* block to see if the condition is satisfied there. Hence you can execute a certain set of code based on multiple conditions.

Syntax:
if(condition1)
    //code to be executed if condition1 is true
elsif (condition2)
    //code to be executed if condition2 is true
else (condition3)
    //code to be executed if condition3 is true
end

Example:

```
Path => /koresol.com-if_elsif.rb
puts  "Enter price"
price = gets.chomp.to_i
if price < 50
   puts "Get Eccomerce Related Services"
elsif price >= 50 && price <= 60
   puts "Get Android App Related Services."
elsif price > 60
   puts "Get iOS App Related Services."
end
```

Output: Now execute the above ruby file, and you would see the output as:

```
$ ruby koresol.com-if-elsif.rb
Enter price
55
Get Android App Related Services
```

Ternary statement

The Ruby **Ternary** statement is a shortened form of *if* statement where it evaluates an expression and if true executes a statement and if false executes another statement.

Syntax:
    test-expression? if-true-expression : if-false-expression

Example:

```
Path => /koresol.com-ternary_statement.rb
puts "Enter price"
price = gets.chomp.to_i
status = (price > 300 ? true : false);
puts status
```

Output: Now execute the above ruby file, and you would see the output as:

```
$ ruby koresol.com-ternary_statement.rb
Enter price
400
true
```

DAY 3

case Statement

Loops And Iterations

DAY 3

case Statement

Ruby case statement is similar to switch in other programming languages. In Ruby, you use *"case"* instead of "switch" and use *"when"* instead of "case." When you need to execute a piece of code matching multiple conditions, then you go for the case statement.

Syntax:
    case expression
       [when expression [, expression ...] [then]
       code]...
    [else
      code]
    end

Example:

```ruby
Path => /koresol.com-case_statement.rb
print "Enter required Service:"
service_name = gets.chomp
case service_name
when "Eccomerce"
    puts "Koresol develops Eccomerce software"
when "Android"
    puts "Koresol develops Android application"
when "iOS"
    puts "Koresol develops iOS application"
else
    puts "Please Enter Correct Service"
end
```

Output: Now execute the above ruby file, and you would see the output as:

```
$ ruby koresol.com-case_statement.rb
Enter required Service: iOS
Koresol develops iOS application
```

Loops And Iterations

for loop

If you need to execute a statement for a fixed number of iterations, then you can use Ruby *for* loop. It iterates a loop for a specific range of numbers. Ruby *for* loop will execute once for each element in the expression.

Syntax:
 for variable [, variable ...] in expression [do]
   code
 end

Example:

```
Path => /koresol.com-for_loop.rb
print "Enter required quantity: "
qty = gets.chomp.to_i
for quantity in 1..qty do
     puts quantity
end
```

Output: Now execute the above ruby file, and you would see the output as:

```
$ ruby koresol.com-for_loop.rb
Enter required quantity: 3
1
2
3
```

while loop

The Ruby *while* loop is used to iterate a program several times. If you need to execute a statement several times until the condition is not satisfied, the while loop is used. Ruby *while* loop executes a condition while a condition is true. Once the condition becomes false, *while* loop stops its execution.

Syntax:

    while conditional [do]
        code
    end

Example:

```
Path => /koresol.com-while_loop.rb
puts  "Enter order number"
order_number = gets.chomp.to_i
while order_number > 0
     puts order_number
     order_number -= 1
end
```

Output: Now execute the above ruby file, and you would see the output as:

```
$ ruby koresol.com-while_loop.rb
Enter order number
3
3
2
1
```

do while loop

The ***do while*** loop is similar to the ***while*** loop as it is also used to execute a part of a program multiple times. The only difference is the program will execute at least once as the condition is specified at the end of the code.

Syntax:

```
loop do
    #code to be executed
   break if booleanExpression
   end
```
Loop will break when condition is not satisfied

Example:

```
Path => /koresol.com-do_while.rb
loop do
  puts "Enter Company Name"
  company = gets.chomp
  if company != 'koresol'
     break
  end
end
```
Output: Now execute the above ruby file, and you would see the output as:

```
$ ruby koresol.com-do_while.rb
Enter Company Name
koresol
Enter Company Name
tcs
```

until loop

The Ruby ***until*** loop runs until the given condition is true. It exits the loop only when the condition is true. It is pretty much opposite of the ***while*** loop, where it executes till the condition is false whereas the ***until*** loop executes till the condition becomes true.

Syntax:
```
until conditional
   code
end
```

Example:
```
Path => /koresol.com-until_loop.rb
order_id=1

until  order_id == 3
     puts order_id
     order_id += 1
end
```
Output: Now execute the above ruby file, and you would see the output as:
```
$ ruby koresol.com-until_loop.rb
1
2
```

break statement

When you need to terminate a loop, a Ruby ***break*** statement is used. It is generally used in a while loop to terminate the loop when the condition becomes true. It is called from inside the loop.

Syntax:
```
loop do
   #code to be executed
   break if booleanExpression
end
```

Example:

```
Path => /koresol.com-break_statement.rb
order_id = 1
while true
    if order_id*4 == 16
       break
    end
       puts order_id*4
       order_id += 1
end
```

Output: Now execute the above ruby file, and you would see the output as:

```
$ ruby koresol.com-break_statement.rb
Enter order id
4
8
12
```

next statement

When you need to skip the loop's next iteration, the Ruby *next* statement is used. Once it executes the *next* statement, the iteration will be stopped. The Ruby *next* statement is similar to continue in other programming languages.

Syntax:
    if (condition)
      //code to be executed
    next
    end

Example:

```
Path => /koresol.com-next_statement.rb
for service_id in 5...10
    if service_id == 7 then
        next
    end
    puts service_id
end
```

Output: Now execute the above ruby file, and you would see the output as:

```
$ ruby koresol.com-next_statement.rb
5
6
8
9
```

redo statement

Ruby *redo* statement is used to repeat the current iteration of the loop. The *redo* statement is executed without evaluating the loop's condition. The *redo* statement is used inside a loop.

Syntax:
    while condition [do]
      redo if (condition)
    end

Example:

Path => /koresol.com-redo_statement.rb
product_id = 0

while(product_id < 4)
   puts product_id
   product_id +=1
   redo if product_id == 4
end

Output: Now execute the above ruby file, and you would see the output as:

$ ruby koresol.com-redo_statement.rb
0
1
2
3
4

Above example will Prints output *"01234"* instead of *"0123"*

DAY 4

Classes

Methods

OOPs Concepts

Day 4

Classes

Ruby is an objected oriented language and hence involves *classes* and *objects*. A class is the blueprint from which different objects are created. It is the class which defines what data an *object* can contain and how it can behave. Say for example, take a vehicle and every vehicle is comprised of wheels, tank capacity, horsepower, mileage, etc. These characteristics of the vehicle form the data members of the class "vehicle." Differentiation between two vehicles can be understood based on these characteristics only.

A vehicle can also have its own functions like driving, braking, and speeding, etc. these functions also become data members of the class. Hence you say that a class is composed of both characteristics and functions.

When you define a class in Ruby, it always starts with a keyword *class* followed by the class name. The *class* name should always start with a capital letter, and the end of the class is determined by the end keyword.

Syntax:
class ClassName
   code...
end

Example:

```
Path => /koresol.com-classes.rb
class   Company
    def   set_product(product_name)
        @product_name = product_name
    end
end
```

Creating object

Create **objects** in Ruby by calling the *new* method of the class. The *new* method is a predefined method in the Ruby library and objects are instances of the class.

Syntax:
objectName = className.new

Example:

```
Path => /koresol.com-classes_object.rb
class   Company
    def   initialize (product_name)
        @product_name = product_name
    end
 end
 company = Company.new("Koresol Software LLP")
```

Constructors - initialize

When a new object is created and if it contains a method *initialize*, it will be automatically called. It is good to include an initialize method to set the value of an object's instance variables.

Example:

```
Path => /koresol.com-constructor.rb
class   Company
    def initialize(product_price, product_description)
        @price = product_price
        @description = product_description
    end
end
```

Methods

When you want to combine a set of statement, again and again, you write a method and just call the method instead of writing the same set of code again and again. It is similar to a function in other programming languages.

Defining Method

We need to define a method before we start using it. It is defined with the **def** keyword followed by the method name. The **end** keyword denotes the end of the method. Methods name should always start with a lowercase letter. Otherwise, it may be misunderstood as a constant.

Syntax:
def methodName
    code...
end

Example:

```
Path => /koresol.com-method.rb
class Company
   def get_company_name
       puts "Koresol Software LLP."
   end
end
```

Instance Methods

Instance methods are also defined using the ***def*** keyword and one can use this method only using a class instance only.

Example:

```
Path => /koresol.com-instance_method.rb
class   Service
   def   initialize(service_price)
      @service_prices = service_price
   end
   def   get_service_price
      10 * @service_prices
   end
 end
 # create an object
service = Service.new(10)
# call instance methods
service_cost  = service.get_service_price()
puts "Price Of Service :#{service_cost}"
```

Output: Now execute the above ruby file, and you would see the output as:

```
$ ruby koresol.com-instance_method.rb
Price Of Service:100
```

OOPs Concepts

Ruby is a complete object oriented programming (OOP) language, and everything in Ruby is an object. Numbers, strings, or even a class is seen as an object in Ruby, as the whole of Ruby language is built only on the concepts of objects and data. OOP is a programming concept that uses objects and their interactions to design applications and computer programs.

Following are some of basic concepts in OOPs:
Encapsulation
Polymorphism
Inheritance

Encapsulation: Encapsulation is the process of combining data and functions inside a single class, and the data cannot be accessed directly. The data is accessed only through the functions present inside the class. Hence, Encapsulation ensures data hiding or protecting data from data manipulation.

Polymorphism: It means one name having different forms. In other words, a single function behaves in different forms.

Inheritance: Inheritance is the process of acquiring a property of another class. Take for example a child inheriting the property of their parents.

Inheritance

New classes are created using predefined classes in Inheritance. The newly created classes are called derived classes, and the classes from which they are derived are called base classes. Inheritance code can be reused again and again and hence reduces the complexity of the program to a great extent. Ruby does not support multiple levels of inheritance. Instead it supports mixins.

When you need to take most of the behavior of the parent class, but just need to do some modifications, you can use the super keyword to access the superclass inside the subclass.

Let's create a *class Company* and also create a subclass called *Software_Company*.

Example:

```ruby
Path => /koresol.com-inheritance.rb

class Company
attr_accessor :service_name
attr_reader   :service_cost
@@current_services = []
  def self.create_with_attributes(service_cost, service_name)
       company =  self.new(service_cost)
       company.service_name = service_name
       return company
  end
  def initialize( service_cost, service_name =
    "Android")
    @service_cost =  service_cost
    @service_name = service_name
    @@current_services << self
    puts "A new service has been instantiated"
  end
  def service_cost
    @service_cost
  end
  def service_name
    "The service_name is #{@service_name}."
  end
end
```

```ruby
class Software_Company  <   Company
  def service_cost
    parent_service_cost =  super
    return "Service Cost #{parent_service_cost}"
  end
end
software_company =
Software_Company.create_with_attributes("1000",
"Eccomerce Website Development")
puts software_company.service_cost
puts software_company.class
puts software_company.service_name
```

Output: Now execute the above ruby file, and you would see the output as:

```
$ ruby koresol.com-inheritance.rb
A new service has been instantiated.
Service Cost 1000
Software_Company
The service_name is Eccomerce Website Development
```

We use the **<** *symbol* to signify that the *Software_Company* class is inheriting from the *Company* class. This means that all of the methods in the *Company* class are available to the *Software_Company* class for use.

Take a close look at *last fourth line* of above ruby file, *create_with_attributes* is not defined within *Software_Company* class but still available to use because it inherits *Company* class, which has a definition for *create_with_attributes*. Same holds true for other attributes and methods of parent class, which are available for use in child class.

Day 5

Ruby Overriding Methods

Modules

Array

Day 5

Overriding Methods

Method overriding is the concept of replacing a method of a *parent class* inside a subclass. The implementation in the *subclass* overrides (replaces) the implementation in the superclass.

Example:

```ruby
Path => /koresol.com-overriding.rb
class Company
   def print_company_name
      puts "In class Company."
   end
end
```

```ruby
class Softwarecompany < Company
    def print_company_name
        puts "In class Software Company."
    end
end
softwarecompany = Softwarecompany.new
softwarecompany.print_company_name
```

Output: Now execute the above ruby file, and you would see the output as:

```
$ ruby koresol.com-overriding.rb
In class Software Company
```

Usage of super

The *super* keyword is used for overriding method in a subclass to execute the parent method and modify or add to any of its input. You use a *super* keyword without any arguments to the parent of the *current object* to invoke a method of the same name. The parent method passes all the arguments that are passed to the method from which the parent method is called using the *super* keyword.

Example:

```ruby
Path => /koresol.com-superclass.rb
class Product
 attr_reader :sell_price, :quantity, :cost_price
  def initialize(sell_price = 100)
      @quantity = 4
      @cost_price = 90
      @sell_price = sell_price
  end
end
class Digital_Product < Product
   def initialize(sell_price)
      super
      @cost_price = 100
   end
end
digital_product = Digital_Product.new(120)
puts  digital_product.sell_price
puts digital_product.quantity
puts digital_product.cost_price
product = Product.new
puts product.sell_price
puts product.quantity
puts product.cost_price
```

Output: Now execute the above ruby file, and you would see the output as:

```
$ ruby koresol.com-superclass.rb
120
4
100
100
4
90
```

Modules

A Module is a collection of methods and constants like classes. But unlike classes, they cannot be instantiated. Modules are similar to classes as they are a combination of methods, class definitions, constants, and even other modules. They are also defined like how classes are defined. As you cannot create objects or subclasses using modules, there is no *module* hierarchy of inheritance.

Modules mainly serve two purposes:
They help in preventing name clashes and also act as namespaces
They help the mixin facility to share the functionality between two classes

Syntax:

>   module ModuleName
>   statement1
>   statement2
>   ....
>   end

Module name should start with a capital letter.

Example:

```
Path => /koresol.com-module.rb
module Product
   CONST = 1
   def print_product_name
       #   ...
   end
end
puts Product.class
puts Product.constants
puts Product.instance_methods
```

Output: Now execute the above ruby file, and you would see the output as:

```
$ ruby koresol.com-module.rb
Module
CONST
print_product_name
```

Array

When you want to store single/multiple objects like integers, numbers, strings, you can use an *array*. Array is an object that is used to **store other objects**. It is created by including ***values separated by a comma*** enclosed in square brackets. [1, 2,3] is a simple *array* that holds three numbers. It can even hold all kinds of objects like strings, numbers inside a ***single array***.

Accessing Array Element

It's indexing start with 0 and the negative index with -1 from the end of the array. So for example, 0 represents the first element of the array and -1 represents the last element of the *array*.

i. The ***length*** method will return the total element of the array.
ii. The ***first*** and ***last*** method will return first and last element of an array respectively.
iii. To access a particular element of an array, ***at*** method can be used.
iv. To ***reverse*** the array, reverse method is used.
v. The ***drop*** method in ruby is just opposite to the take method. It returns all the elements after the elements that have been dropped.
vi. To add elements to an array, you can use the ***push*** method.

Example:

```
Path => /koresol.com-array.rb
service = ["Eccomerce Website Development","iOS Application Development", "Android Application Development"]
puts service
print "Array Length:"
puts service.length
print "Array First Element:"
puts service.first
print "Array Last Element:"
puts service.last
print "Array Element At Specified Position:"
puts service[1]
print "Reverse Array:"
puts service.reverse
print "Drop Element Of Array:"
puts service.drop(2)
print "Add Element To End Of Array:"
service.push("Mobile Application Development")
puts service
```

Output: Now execute the above ruby file, and you would see the output as:

```
$ ruby koresol.com-array.rb
Eccomerce Website Development
iOS Application Development
Android Application Development
Array Length: 3
Array First Element: Eccomerce Website Development
Array Last Element: Android Application Development
Array Element At Specified Position: iOS Application
Development
Reverse Array: Android Application Development
iOS Application Development
Eccomerce Website Development
Drop Element Of Array: Android Application Development
Add Element To End Of Array: Eccomerce Website
Development
iOS Application Development
Android Application Development
Mobile Application Development
```

Day 6

Hashes

String

Ruby Operators

Math Function

Day 6

Hashes

Hashes also known as associative arrays - are an unordered, object- indexed collection of objects. The only difference between arrays and hashes is that - in arrays, integers are used for indexing the elements, but in hashes, you can use even a string or regular expression for indexing.

So when you want to store a value in a *hash*, you need to provide an index and the value. The value of the *hash* can be retrieved by specifying the key associated with the value. So it's key-value pair. One object is key, and the other object is value.

The example *koresol.com-hash.rb* below uses hash literals: a list of *key => value* pairs between {} braces.

Example:

```
Path => /koresol.com-hash.rb
service = {"service1" => "Eccomerce Website
Development", "service2" => "iOS Application
Development", "service3" => "Android Application
Development", "service4" => "iPhone Application
Development"}
puts service
print  "Get Particular Value Using Key :"
puts service["service2"]
```

Output: Now execute the above ruby file, and you would see the output as:

```
$ ruby koresol.com-hash.rb
{"service1"=>"Eccomerce Website Development",
"service2"=>"iOS Application Development",
"service3"=>"Android Application Development",
"service4"=>"iPhone Application Development"}
Get Particular Value Using Key :iOS Application
Development
```

Hash Methods

A Ruby *hash* has many methods. Some are public class methods and some public instance methods.

Public Class Methods

Method	Description
Hash[object]	Create a new hash with given objects
new(obj)	Return a new empty hash.
try_convert(obj)	Try to convert object into hash.

Public Instance Methods

Method	Description
hsh==other_hash	Two hashes are equal if they contain the same key and value pair.
hsh[key]	Retrieve value from the respective key.
hsh[key] = value	Associates new value to the given key.
assoc(obj)	Compare objects inside the hash.
Clear	Remove all key value pair from hash.

Method	Description
default = obj	Sets the default value.
delete(key)	Delete key value pair.
Each	Call block once for each key in hash.
empty?	Return true if hash contains no key value pair.
eql>(other)	Return true if hash and other both have same content
fetch(key[, default])	Return value from hash for a given key.
has_key?(key)	Return true if given key is present in hash.
has_value?(value)	Return true if given value is present in hash for a key.
include?(key)	Return true if given key is present in hash.
compare_by_identity	Compare hash keys based on their identity.
compare_by_identity	Return true if hash compare its keys by their identity.

String

In Ruby, when character are strung together, they form Strings. In simple words - they are sequences of characters. String can be a letter, a word, a sentence, a paragraph, or even several paragraphs.

Multiline string
When it comes to handling strings in Ruby, it is pretty simple. To create a multiline string in Ruby, you need to enter the *string* within double quotes. You can also use a % character and enclose the *string* within to create a multiline *string*.

Example:

```
Path => /koresol.com-multiline_string.rb
  puts "
product
order
lineitem
checkout"
puts %/
product
order
lineitem
checkout/
```

Output: Now execute the above ruby file, and you would see the output as:

```
$ ruby koresol.com-multiline_string.rb
product
order
lineitem
checkout
product
order
lineitem
checkout
```

String compare

Ruby strings can be compared with three operators:

- With **= =** operator: Returns *true* or *false*
- With *eql?* Operator: Returns *true* or *false*
- With *casecmp* method: Returns 0 if matched or 1 if not matched

String concatenation

When you want to join multiple strings into a single string, you can go for Ruby **string concatenation**. You can join more than one string to form a single string by concatenating them. There are various ways to concatenate multiple strings into single string.

- using **+** method
  e.g. myString = "Welcome " + "to " + "Ruby!"
- using **<<** method
  e.g. myString = "Welcome " << "to " << "Ruby!"
- using *concat* method
  e.g. myString = "Welcome ".concat("to ").concat("Ruby!")

String length

String ***length*** returns the number of bytes in a string or the count of the characters in a string. Here's a Ruby method call:

company.length

String reverse

The string ***reverse*** method allows you to reverse the string provided. Ruby method call:

company.reverse

String downcase

When you need a string only in lowercase letters, you can use the String ***downcase*** method. It returns a copy of the string with all the uppercase letters replaced with lowercase letters. It only returns a copy of the string, and the original variable is not changed. This operation is locale insensitive as only the characters "A-Z" are affected.

company.downcase

String empty?

To check if a string is empty? You can use the string empty method. It returns true if the length of the string is Zero.

company.empty?

String replace

To replace a string with another string, you can use string ***replace***.

Example:

```ruby
Path => /koresol.com-string_operation.rb
puts "String Compare"
puts "ecommerce" == "ecommerce"
puts "android" == "web"
puts "23" == "32"
puts "ios".eql? "ios"
puts "12".eql? "12"
puts "String Concat"
statement = "Ruby Tutorial" + " from KORESOL."
puts statement
statement = "Ruby Tutorial" " from KORESOL." puts statement
statement = "Ruby Tutorial" << " from KORESOL."
puts statement
statement="Ruby Tutorial".concat("from KORESOL.")
puts statement
puts "String Length."
company = "KORESOL SOFTWARE LLP."
puts company.length
puts "String Reverse."
puts company.reverse
puts "String Downcase."
puts company.downcase
puts "String Empty."
puts company.empty?
puts "String Replace."
puts company.replace "Koresol."
```

Output: Now execute the above ruby file, and see the output:

```
$ ruby koresol.com-string_operation.rb
String Compare
true
false
false
true
true
String Concat
Ruby Tutorial from KORESOL.
Ruby Tutorial from KORESOL.
Ruby Tutorial from KORESOL.
Ruby Tutorial from KORESOL.
String Length
21
String Reverse
.PLL ERAWTFOS LOSEROK
String Downcase
koresol software llp.
String Empty.
false
String Replace.
Koresol.
```

Ruby Operators

Unary operator

Unary operators expect a single operand to run on, as shown below:

Operator	Description
!	Boolean NOT
~	Bitwise complement
+	Unary plus

Now, let's take a look at how these operators work with an example. Create a ***koresol.com-unary_operator.rb*** and write the following code in it:

Example:

```
puts (~4)
puts (~-4)
puts (!true)
puts (!false)
```

Output: Now execute the above ruby file, and you would see the output as:

```
$ ruby koresol.com-unary_operator.rb
-5
3
false
true
```

Arithmetic operator

Arithmetic operators take numerical values as operands and return a single value.

Operator	Description
+	Adds value from both sides of the operator.
-	Subtracts value from both sides of the operator.
/	Divides left side operand with right side operand
*	Multiply values from both sides of the operator.
**	Right side operand becomes the exponent of the left side operand.
%	Divide left side operand with the right side operand returning remainder

In file *koresol.com-arithmetic_operator.rb*, write the following code.

```
Path =>/koresol.com-arithmetic_operator.rb
puts    ("add operator")
puts    (15 + 20)
puts    ("subtract operator")
puts    (40 - 15)
puts    ("multiply operator")
puts    (5 * 8)
puts    ("division operator")
puts    (36 / 6)
puts    ("exponential operator")
puts    (7 ** 2)
puts    ("modulo operator")
puts    (26 % 4)
```

Output: Now execute the above ruby file, and you would see the output as:

```
$ ruby koresol.com-arithmetic_operator.rb
add operator
35
subtract operator
25
multiply operator
40
division operator
6
exponential operator
49
modulo operator
2
```

Comparison operator

Comparison operators compare two operands. Below mentioned are Ruby Comparison operators:

Operator	Description
==	Equal operator.
!=	Not equal operator
>	Left operand is greater than right operand
<	Right operand is greater than left operand
>=	Left operand is greater than or equal to right operand
<=	Right operand is greater than or equal to left operand
<=>	Combined comparison operator
.eql?	Checks for equality and type of the operands

Example:

```
Path => /koresol.com-comparison_operator.rb
puts   ("Comparison Operator")
puts   (5==3)
puts   (5!=3)
puts   (5>3)
puts   (5<3)
puts   (5>=3)
puts   (5<=3)
```

Output: Now execute the above ruby file, and you would see the output as:

```
$ ruby koresol.com-comparison_operator.rb
 Comparison Operator
 false
 true
 true
 false
 true
 false
```

Math Functions

The *Math* module contains "methods/functions" for basic trigonometric and transcendental functions.

In Ruby, we invoke built-in *Math* functions, such as - *sqrt* returns a square root. The *sin*, *cos* and *tan* methods relate parts of a triangle. There are two constants: *PI* and *E*.

sqrt(x)
Returns the non-negative square root of x.

cbrt(x)
Returns the cube root of x.

log10(x)
Returns the base 10 logarithm of x.

log(x, base)
Returns the logarithm of x. If additional second argument is given, it will be the base of logarithm. Otherwise it is e (for the natural logarithm).

Example:

```
Path => /koresol.com-math_function.rb
print "Square root of number : "
puts Math.sqrt(64)
print "Cube root of number : "
puts Math.cbrt(8)
print "Logarithm value of number : "
puts Math.log(1)
print "Logarithm value to the base 10 : "
puts Math.log10(10)
print "Give value of PI Constant : "
puts Math::PI
print "Give value of E Constant : "
puts Math::E
print "Trigonometric functions: "
puts Math::sin(0)
puts Math::cos(0)
puts Math::tan(0)
```

Output: Now execute the above ruby file, and you would see the output as:

```
$ ruby koresol.com-math_function.rb
Square root of number: 8.0
Cube root of number: 2.0
Logarithm value of number: 0.0
Logarithm value to the base 10: 1.0
Give value of PI Constant: 3.141592653589793
Give value of E Constant: 2.718281828459045
Trigonometric functions: 0.0
1.0
0.0
```

<u>Day 7</u>

Exceptions

Variable Interpolation

Comments

Yield Statement And Block

Day 7

Exceptions

Exception handling is very important in writing programs as you never know when something will break. So you always be prepared for the worst and need to have proper exception handling routines written in your program. These exceptions tell the program what to do if something goes wrong. Ruby generally terminates when something goes wrong, but you can instruct Ruby to do something when a failure happens.

An exception handler ensures whether to continue with the execution of the code in some other method or exit the program gracefully without terminating and informing the user. An exception is a special kind of *object*, an instance of the class *Exception* or a descendant of that *class*.

Built-in subclasses of exception are as follows:
>	NoMemoryError
>	ScriptError
>	SecurityError
>	SignalException
>	StandardError
>	SystenExit
>	SystemStackError
>	fatal - impossible to rescue

Example:

```
Path => /koresol.com-exception.rb
class Excep
   def raise_exception
      puts "Inside raise-Exception."
      raise "Exception raised"
      puts "Outside raise-Exception"
   end
end
excep = Excep.new
excep.raise_exception
```

Output: Now execute the above ruby file, and you would see the output as:

```
$ ruby koresol.com-exception.rb
Inside raise-Exception.
koresol.com-exception.rb:4:in `raise_exception':
Exception raised (RuntimeError)
	from koresol.com-exception.rb:9:in `<main>'
```

Handling an exception

Handling exception in Ruby is pretty much simple as you just need to enclose the exception handling code inside a ***begin/rescue/end*** block. It is similar to ***if else*** statement, where it executes something if it sees an error or continues with the original function. The exception class handles all types of problems in the code including runtime errors, syntax errors or incorrect type handling, etc. The ***begin/rescue*** block is where you handle errors and if no problem, continue with the original execution.

Example:

```
Path => /koresol.com-exception_handling.rb
class Excep
   def raise_exception
      begin
         puts "Inside raise-Exception."
         raise "Exception raised"
         puts "Outside raise-Exception"
      rescue
         puts "Inside rescued."
      end
      puts "Outside begin block."
   end
end
excep = Excep.new
excep.raise_exception
```

Output: Now execute the above ruby file, and you would see the output as:

```
$ ruby koresol.com-exception_handling.rb
Inside raise-Exception.
Inside rescued.
Outside begin block.
```

Variable Interpolation

Variable interpolation in Ruby is about replacing the values of variables in **string literals**. The *variable* name is put between # tag enclosed inside *{* and *}* characters.

Example:

```
Path => /koresol.com-interpolation.rb
name = "Koresol"
city = "Pune"
puts "#{name} is located in #{city}"
```

Output: Now execute the above ruby file, and you would see the output as:

```
$ ruby koresol.com-interpolation.rb
Koresol is located in Pune
```

Comments

In your source code, you can add *comments* wherever needed to make the code more understandable when referenced in the future. Many source code examples provided in this book also comes with a lot of *comments* added. The ruby interpreter ignores all text on a line that is placed after a *hash #*. Say for example, any text that follows the # tag is ignored, and the interpreter moves to the next line. But in case you need to add multi-line *comments*, you need place a *=begin* at the start of the comment and then *=end* at the end of the comment. See the example below to understand the usage of comments easily. Comments are an important aspect of coding and are often regarded as a good habit to add comments about the usage of the function or class, date created, name of the person, etc.

Example:

```
Path => /koresol.com-comment.rb
puts "Welcome to Koresol's Ruby tutorial"
# Single line comment
=begin
This is a
multiline
 comment
=end
```

Output: Now execute the above ruby file, and you would see the output as:

```
$ ruby koresol.com-comment.rb
Welcome to Koresol's Ruby tutorial
```

yield Statement

The yield statement

To call a block within a method with a value, you can use the *yield* statement.

Example:

```
Path => /koresol.com-yield_statement.rb
def service
    puts "Koresol develops eccomerce software"
    yield
    puts "Koresol develops android applications"
    yield
end
service { puts "Koresol is software company" }
```

Output: Now execute the above ruby file, and you would see the output as:

```
$ ruby koresol.com-yield_statement.rb
Koresol develops eccomerce software
Koresol is software company
Koresol develops android applications
Koresol is software company
```

BEGIN and END block

BEGIN is used to indicate that the file is being loaded and the ***END*** block is used to indicate that the file has been loaded.

Example:

```
Path => /koresol.com-begin_end_block.rb
BEGIN {
   puts "Welcome to Koresol's Ruby Tutorial."
}
END {
   puts "Congratulations, you completed Koresol's Ruby tutorial."
}
puts "You completed tutorial partially."
```

Output: Now execute the above ruby file, and you would see the output as:

```
$ ruby koresol.com-begin_end_block.rb
Welcome To Koresol's Ruby Tutorial.
You completed tutorial partially."
Congratulations, you completed Koresol's Ruby tutorial.
```

Upcoming RAILS Tutorial

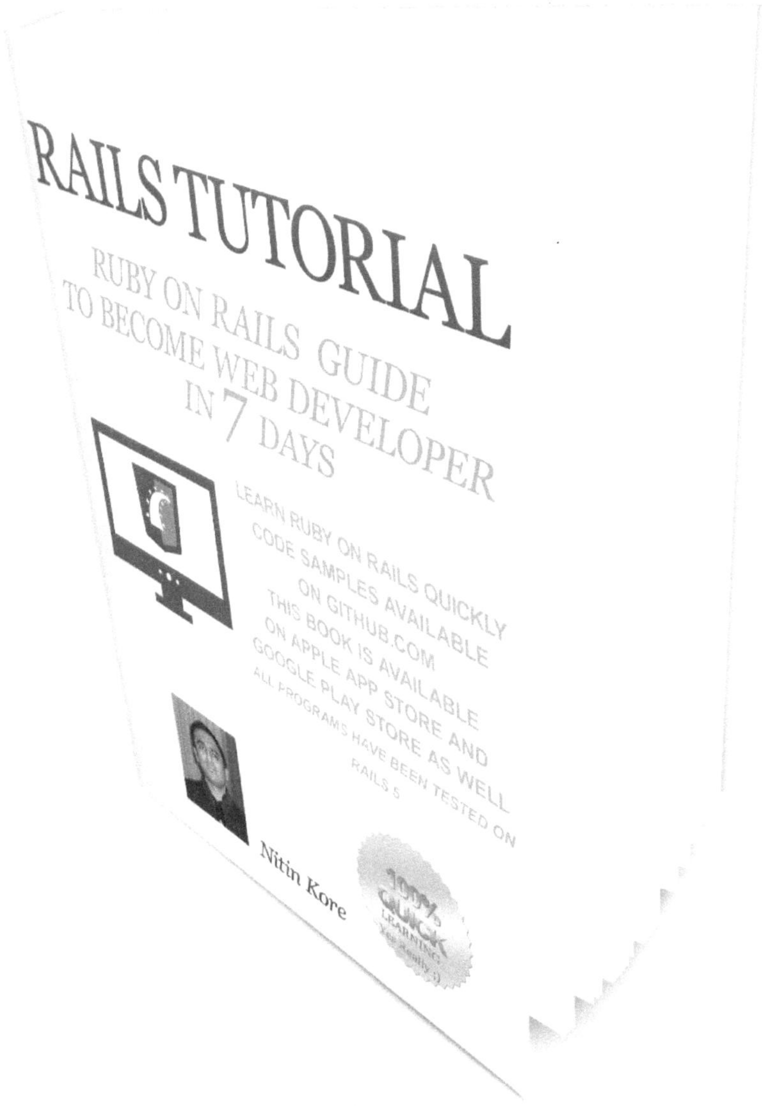

www.ingramcontent.com/pod-product-compliance
Lightning Source LLC
Chambersburg PA
CBHW020452220526
45464CB00002B/965